# DON MEE CHOI

DN

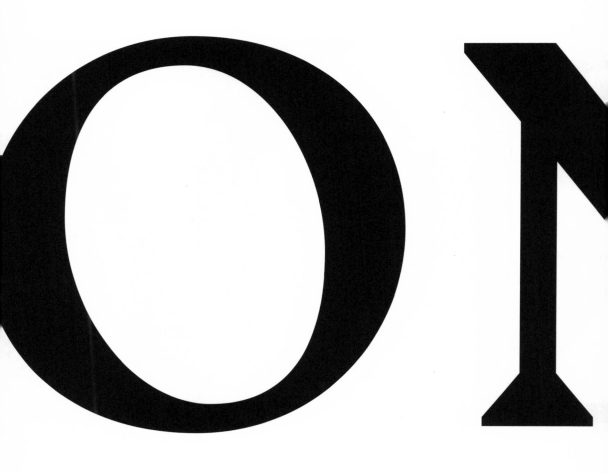

WAVE BOOKS

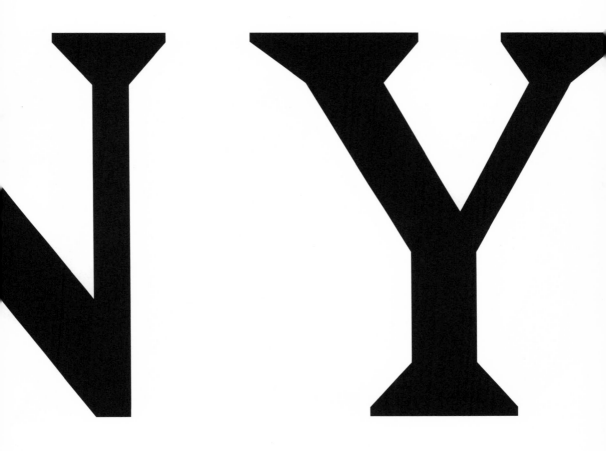

SEATTLE & NEW YORK

Published by Wave Books

www.wavepoetry.com

Copyright © 2020 by Don Mee Choi

All rights reserved

Wave Books titles are distributed to the trade by

Consortium Book Sales and Distribution

Phone: 800-283-3572 / SAN 631-760X

Library of Congress Cataloging-in-Publication Data

Names: Choi, Don Mee, author.

Title: DMZ colony / Don Mee Choi.

Description: First edition. | Seattle : Wave Books, [2020]

Identifiers: LCCN 2019030061

ISBN 9781940696966

ISBN 9781940696959 (trade paperback)

Classification: LCC PS3603.H65 A6 2020 | DDC 818/.608—dc2 3

LC record available at https://lccn.loc.gov/2019030061

Designed by Crisis

Printed in Canada

9  8  7  6  5  4  3  2

Wave Books 083

*for all the birds and children in flight*

**Raúl Zurita:**

*MY GOD IS WOUND*

*—written in the sky—*

*New York—June 1982*

trans. by Anna Deeny Morales

from *Sky Below*


*The night sings, sings, sings, sings*

*She sings, sings, sings beneath the earth*

trans. by Daniel Borzutzky

from *Songs for His Disappeared Love*


**Aimé Césaire:**

*rise*

*rise*

*rise*

*I follow you who are imprinted on my ancestral white cornea*

*Rise sky licker*

trans. by A. James Arnold and Clayton Eshleman

from *The Original 1939 Notebook of a Return to the Native Land*

the waist of a nation

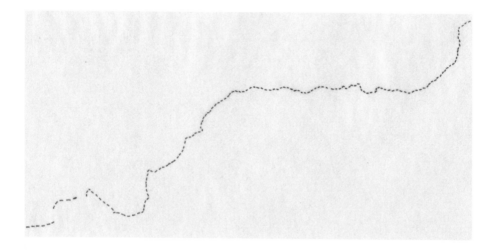

the 38th parallel north

The Korean Demilitarized Zone is approximately 160 miles long and 2.5 miles wide. The DMZ runs across the 38th parallel, a division created after World War II, with the end of the 35-year-long Japanese occupation of Korea. The US occupied the south, and the Soviet Union the north. The US still occupies South Korea with military installations, bases, and troops. The Korean border is one of the most militarized borders in the world.

------------------------------------------------- Saint Louis, Missouri

38.648056 north

On February 23, 2018, the day of my poetry reading with Daniel Borzutzky at the Pulitzer Arts Foundation, I walked across Forest Park in Saint Louis, Missouri. I was heading toward the Saint Louis Art Museum. I heard a kind of muted, distant calling, a polyphony of cries. Because I had never heard the flock calls of snow geese before, I was baffled by the flood of sound, seemingly from nowhere and everywhere. Instinctively, I turned my head from side to side, then up. My head, tilted back, triggered vertigo, a common symptom of Ménière's disease. My ears flapped about dizzyingly like a sparrow and followed the migrating snow geese above. The geese promptly instructed me, a chorus:

... return ... return ... return ... return ... return ... return ...
... return ... return ... return ... return ... return ... return ...
... return ... return ... return ... return ... return ... return ...

Then they flew even higher, out of my ears' reach. The snow geese must have felt sorry for the homesick sparrow from a faraway place, for they dropped me a little line from the sky.

SEE YOU AT DMZ

Alone again, I could only chirp to myself. Translator for hire! Hire, hire me.

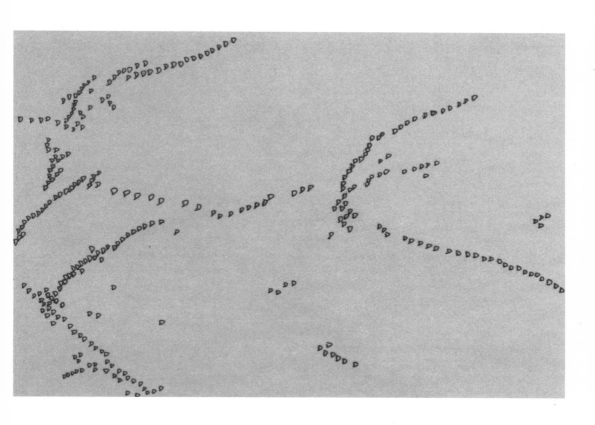

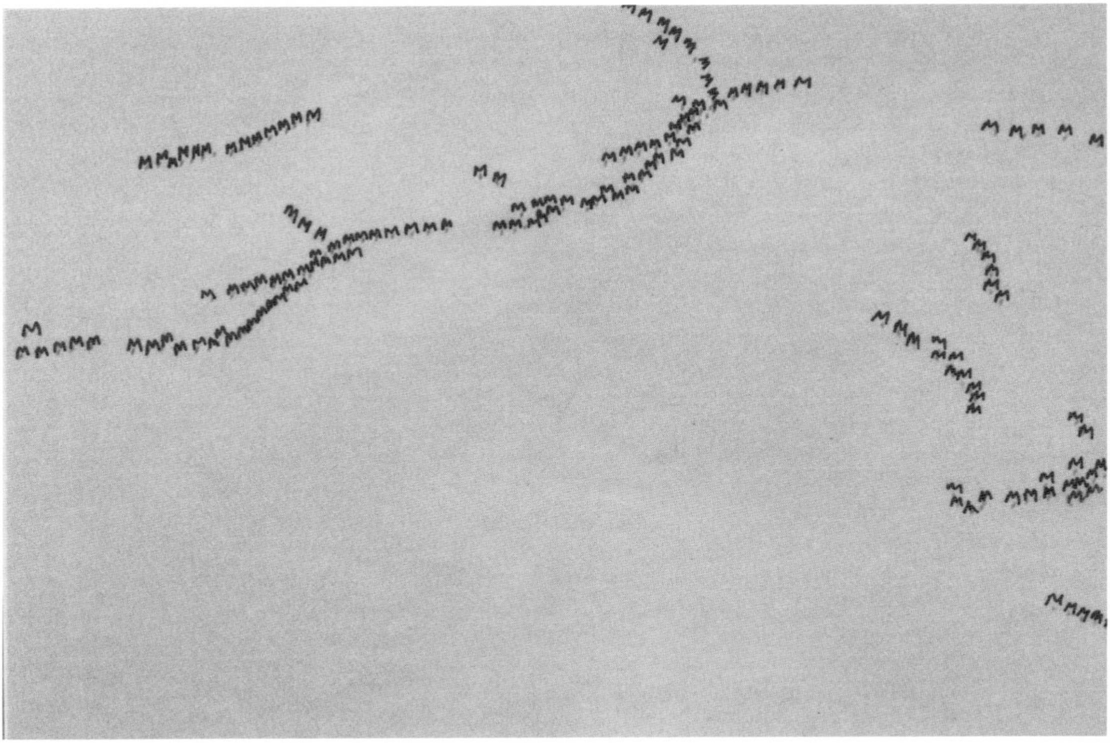

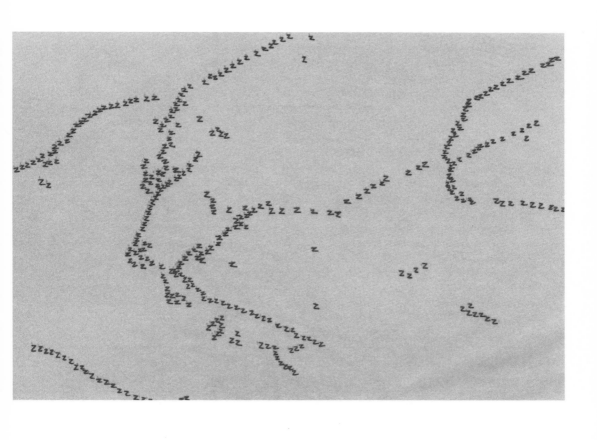

# WINGS

# OF

# RETURN

I grew up in South Korea during the US-backed military dictatorship. I was born a year after General Park Chung Hee led a military coup and came into power. My father filmed the day of martial-law declaration in front of Seoul City Hall. Back then, he worked as a freelance photojournalist for UPI. The saluting lieutenant general is one of Park's collaborators. The man in the background below the window, holding a small camera in front of his face, is most likely a police or intelligence officer. My father is at the bottom left, holding his film camera. After the parade, my father was briefly taken into the building where he stood face-to-face with Park. My father said that he was not afraid. He said he wasn't afraid of Syngman Rhee, the previous dictatorial president, either. He wasn't afraid of anything then, he said; instead, he complained to Park about the censorship of the news. That day his film made it out of Kimpo Airport to Tokyo, and his news footage appeared worldwide. Because I was an infant, I have no memory of this infamous day except through my father's memory. Memory's memory. Memory's child. My memory lives inside my father's camera, the site where my memory was born, where my retina and my father's overlap. When I was old enough, I always accompanied my mother to the airport to greet my father, who returned home every three to five months from Vietnam. Overlapping memory always longs for return, the return of memory.

What I remember about my childhood are the children, no older than I, who used to come around late afternoons begging for leftovers, even food that had gone sour. The drills at school in preparation for attacks by North Korea kept me anxious at night. I feared separation from my family due to the ever-pending war. I feared what my mother feared—my brother being swept up in protests and getting arrested and tortured. Our radio was turned off at night in case we were suspected of being North Korean sympathizers. At school, former North Korean spies came to give talks on the evil leader of North Korea. I stood at bus stops to see if I could spot any North Korean spies, but all I could spot were American GIs. My friends and I waved to them and called them Hellos. In our little courtyard, I skipped rope and played house with my paper dolls among big, glazed jars of fermented veggies and spicy, pungent pastes. I feared the shadows they cast along the path to the outhouse. Stories of abandoned infant girls always piqued my interest, so I imagined that the abandoned babies might be inside the jars. Whenever I obeyed the shadows, I saw tiny, floating arms covered in mold. And whenever it snowed, I made tiny snowmen on the lids of the jars. Like rats, children can be happy in darkness. But the biggest darkness of all was the midnight curfew. I didn't know the curfew was a curfew till my family escaped from it in 1972 and landed in Hong Kong. That's how big the darkness was.

In 1980, my father filmed the rising waves of student protests against the dictatorship in Seoul. He also witnessed the brutal military crackdown on the pro-democratic uprising in Gwangju. He believed then that the dictatorship would never end and that it would be too dangerous for us to return home. He sold one of his cameras to pay for surgery when my older brother was injured during his mandatory military service. He gave the South Korean government news footage of a student protest in downtown Seoul he had filmed—from far away, from a rooftop—in exchange for the release of my injured brother from the military and a permit to leave South Korea. He believed that he was saving us from a life of perpetual darkness. In 1983, my family scattered all over, as my mother said. My parents and my younger brother headed to West Germany. My sister remained in Hong Kong, my older brother left for Australia, and I went to the US as a foreign student to complete my degrees in art. In light, we all were ailing from separation and homesickness. In light, we had to find a way to settle down, as my mother said. In light, we lived like birds.

In December 2016, I returned to South Korea. I returned in the guise of a translator, which is to say, I returned as a foreigner. And as a foreigner, I was invisible to most. I flittered about in downtown Seoul searching for my child self that had been left behind long ago. As a foreigner, I understood only the language of wings—the wings on totem animals on old palaces where I used to run around and play. The traditional tiled roofs I grew up beneath had grown wings, as had the mountain peaks behind Gwanghwamun Square. They no longer recognized me in a crowd of other foreigners—tourists, rather. Nevertheless, I went on searching for more wings, my language of return.

# Ahn Hak-sŏp #1

Mr. Ahn was a political prisoner from 1953 to 1995. He currently lives in a farming village within the Civilian Control Zone, on the South Korean side of the DMZ. The CCZ was created by a US Army commander in 1954, after the Korean War, and it remained relatively unpopulated till the 1980s. The new settlements in the CCZ are commonly referred to as "DMZ villages." To enter the DMZ village near the city of Kimpo, west of Seoul, I had to pass a guard post manned by young soldiers. I also observed seemingly endless barbed-wire fencing across the rice fields. Ahn, now in his eighties, remains a North Korean sympathizer. Every time a missile is test-fired in North Korea—usually before or after the massive biannual, joint US and ROK military exercises—Ahn is placed under house arrest. I recorded Ahn and also scribbled in my notebook while listening to his life story at his house on December 23, 2016. I remain a daughter of neocolony.

. . . I was born in Kanghwa province . . . finished my elementary education . . . then the liberation . . . I really thought that Korea was liberated . . . I hid in a den during the day and came out only at night . . . then the liberation . . . I was told that I could come out because we were liberated . . . I felt at the time that really, this really was the world, but it didn't last long . . . soon I was on the wanted list . . . I couldn't attend school regularly . . . in Seoul . . . later Kaesong . . . then the Korean War . . . I was swept here and there during the war . . . I went all the way up north along the Chinese border as the North Korean troops retreated . . . I received orders to go back to Seoul . . . many meanderings . . . a country that's not a country, a divided country . . . I didn't learn English at school . . . I always skipped my English class . . . that's how much I despised America . . . not the people but its government . . . I gained my pro-independence awareness in grade two . . . my teacher was like a madman and whipped us when he realized that we only knew Japanese and didn't know Korean at all . . . when I told my father about it he said that I would understand my teacher when I got older . . . I remember my father listening to the news on the radio about the anti-Japanese independence movement led by Kim Il-sung . . . he was referred to as a general then . . . I remember hearing a faint voice on the radio . . . I wasn't in hiding for any kind of political consciousness or reason . . . during the Japanese occupation my three older brothers were in the Japanese military . . . one stayed in the army, and the other two planned an escape . . . if you didn't speak Japanese then you couldn't get a permit to travel . . . many young women were taken as comfort women and young men were conscripted into the Japanese military or into forced labor . . . so everyone married early . . . my sister-in-law died a few months after giving birth, and I had to find something to feed the baby . . . there was no milk or sugar . . . we were surrounded by rice fields, but the rice was not for us . . . the Japanese took everything, even spoons and chopsticks . . . because one of my brothers escaped my father was constantly arrested and questioned . . . I was wanted too . . . I'd mailed a letter with money to my brothers for their escape . . . one evening my father told me to quickly finish my dinner and go to my aunt's before sunrise . . . like I said I despised America . . . I really thought America liberated us . . . in Incheon when people came out to welcome the Americans they were shot indiscriminately . . . the American troops were not liberators but occupiers . . . I was sixteen in 1946 and began participating in the movement against the US military's occupation . . . I ran errands for the organizers . . . it was after the curfew . . . I was carrying documents from the meeting . . . I ran and threw the documents into the acacia tree and hid in the well . . . the police officer chased me . . . he was a former pro-Japanese collaborator . . . my body was frozen from the cold water even though it was August . . . if the police had gotten hold of the documents the entire Kanghwa would have been on fire . . . I couldn't go home . . . I met with someone who resisted despite being tortured for over a month with water and electricity . . . the stench of puss from his body was unbearable . . . he was beaten so much that all of his skin had blistered . . . he stank of rot . . . his insides must have been rotting too . . . the stench of his body is still deep inside my mind . . . I was arrested in Kaesong . . . I was in school on the second floor . . . a truckload of police arrived for me . . . then I was let out and told to report in every week . . . I returned to Kanghwa . . . drifted here and there . . . had a bad case of dysentery . . . I studied and exercised even in the middle of the night because I knew I would be tortured if I ever got arrested . . . I went to Namp'o, to Sinŭiju, to Ch'osan, and across the Amnok River to China . . . I was instructed to go back to Seoul . . . I mostly studied . . . 1951 . . . Kaesong was attacked . . . 1952 . . . many died . . . I was arrested in 1953 . . . jailed in Seoul . . . I received medical treatment in Taegu . . . I was tortured . . . endless torture . . . I didn't give out any information . . . more torture . . . the guy who was torturing me suddenly stopped and said, Don't be a fool . . . just admit that you are a party member . . . but I was just a foot soldier . . . 1954 . . . I had a trial and was sent to a military prison . . . if you didn't bleed for a day then you had your ancestors to thank for it . . . the soldiers came in morning, afternoon, and night and would point and yell . . . YOU . . . and you had to state your name, age, and your crime right away, and if you didn't they'd beat the shit out of you with a club . . . your head

. . . your back . . . the amount of food we received . . . less than a centimeter of rice in a bowl . . . barely a bite . . . many died from malnutrition . . . I tried to escape . . . but when I tried to run only my mind could run . . . my legs wouldn't move . . . they wouldn't follow me . . . my arms and legs were like matchsticks . . . a bean-sprout soup . . . it would be a miracle if you found even three bean sprouts in the broth . . . even intellectuals became like idiots . . . their families abandoned them . . . under the daily abuse . . . YOU . . . and all they could say was . . . uh . . . uh . . . uh . . . but they could read when ordered to read . . . they just couldn't speak . . . uh . . . uh . . . uh . . . from shock . . . I realized then how important one's surroundings were . . . how important nurture was . . . there were different levels of prisoners . . . one to five, and level five got the most food . . . a medic in charge made a public announcement that even an overweight person who lived on the food rations of level five would die from malnutrition within a year . . . 1956 . . . will you change your political view or not? If not write down your reason . . . those of us who refused to change our political view were beaten . . . twenty to twenty-two of us were packed into a tiny cell that was big enough for only eight people . . . we weren't allowed to lean our backs on the walls either . . . we were deprived of many rights . . . no visitation, no letters, no medical care . . . we were each given a blanket to sleep on . . . this is going to sound like a lie . . . in the morning when we shook the blankets to fold them the dust from the blankets was so thick that it looked as if smoke was coming out of the room . . . that's why we had to keep the door closed . . . when the dust settled it was about 2 millimeters thick . . . I know it sounds like a lie . . . I was going to die one way or the other . . . from the beatings or from getting sick . . . I decided that I wanted to be able to move my body before I died . . . I opened the door . . . the entire prison was on alert . . . the guards thought there was a fire . . . I admitted that I was the one who opened the door . . . I won't say what they did to me . . . I'll leave it up to your imagination . . .

I'll leave it up to your imagination what a DMZ village looks like, what his house looks like, what his dogs look like, how many of his teeth are missing, how fit he still is, how he carefully peels sweet potatoes roasted in his woodstove, how terribly beautiful the Han River looks behind the endless barbed-wire fence, how many soldiers guard the Civilian Control Zone, how he points to the river, how the river connects to the Imjin River, flowing from the north to south, what a country that's not a country looks like, what smoke that's not smoke looks like, how he tilts his gaze sideways when he says I'll leave it up to your imagination, the size of the blisters, whether a political view can be changed or not, whether a divided country is a country or not, what shock sounds like, how this really was the world, how deep the well was, whether the acacia tree was in bloom or not.

# Ahn Hak-sŏp #2

. . . May of 1957 . . . we started a hunger strike . . . there were 367 of us . . . someone said 368 . . . but I know it was 367 . . . we all signed on and organized the strike . . . first round, second round, third round, fourth round . . . we were beaten indiscriminately . . . our hands tied back . . . the guards still used Japanese words . . . lost our consciousness . . . and were thrown into solitary cells . . . threw cold water at us . . . when I woke up I was still alive . . . sounds of torture . . . second round . . . indiscriminate beatings . . . many dropped out . . . after the third and fourth and . . . indiscriminate beatings . . . everybody gave up . . . only 8 of us went all the way . . . we were ready to die . . . when your stomach stays empty for long . . . we were near starved to begin with . . . it churns . . . as if someone's cutting it out . . . my comrade was in so much pain that he passed urine . . . only a few drops . . . nothing in him to come out . . . so we said . . . if you want to live, eat . . . we gave him water . . . in August someone from Central Intelligence came . . . suddenly our food ration was upgraded . . . you could even buy extra food if you had money . . . we could exercise . . . no one died from malnutrition anymore . . . all the prisons nationwide . . . but they kept the pressure on . . . torture . . . indiscriminate beatings . . . for instance . . . if you dropped your chopsticks or rice bowl . . . What's that signal? . . . What's that code? . . . they beat the shit out of us . . . they demanded meaning

 . . . meaning . . . yet meaningless . . . it was impossibly absurd . . . for instance . . . if you accidently dropped your wooden pillow at night . . . You signaled! . . . this comrade of mine was too frail . . . I said I was the one . . . these guys still used the Japanese word for a shotgun . . . my arms were not long enough . . . for a loop . . . for a shotgun to be tied . . . so they did it this way . . .

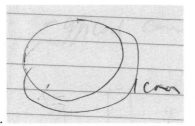

. . . for instance . . . a neocolonial code . . .

. . . for instance . . . an anti-neocolonial code . . .

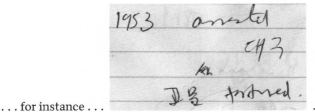

. . . for instance . . .                    . . . impossibly

. . . impossibly a loop

. . . impossibly a ribbon . . . impossibly, impossibly neocolonial . . .

. . . for instance . . .                    . . . indiscriminate signs

. . . meaning, meaning, Mr.

. . . for instance . . . a few drops of urine

. . . impossibly coded

## Ahn Hak-sŏp #3

Then terror came

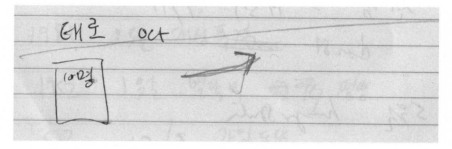

10 prisoners were stuffed into a cell, barely 24.9 square feet, which is 0.000571814
acres to be exact, to be exact is to be stuffed into 24.90821784, to be, terror
in October, in 1971 or 1972
I said to the fellow prisoners this is when we need to keep our heads down
Like I thought, we were rounded up and beaten


Then terror came
We were side by side squeezed into one another
The person behind you had to lean against the wall, then you leaned against him
and the person in front could only sit on your lap
That is how we slept
like spoons
like bean sprouts
Then terror came

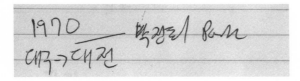

1970 ——— 박정희 Park
대구→대전

Park Chung Hee came

error

to be exact

Then we leaned against him

like spoons

like bean sprouts

Then the task force came:

Central Intelligence

police

pastors

educators

operators

of ideology

to be exact

We never lost any debates with the task force

Operators of

like bean sprouts

of, of, of, of, of

of, of, of, of, of

We knew our position

economically, politically, theoretically

Therefore terror came

You stand up to use the toilet, and they beat you

for standing up without permission

We were transferred from prison to prison


Operators of

spoons

bean sprouts

beat, beat, beat

then everyone came

then terror

then korea

Then we knew
G H 로

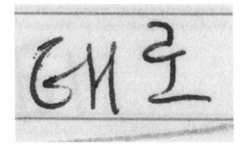

Toward Global Humanity

# Ahn Hak-sŏp #4

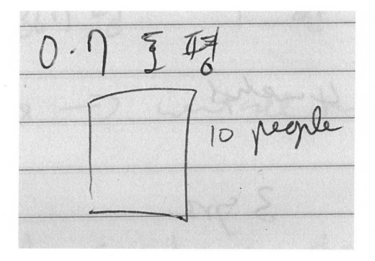

## *24.9082 square feet*

... I'll leave it up to your imagination ... they even shoved 20 people in at one point ... we were beaten when we needed to urinate, defecate ... there was an army lieutenant ... he was arrested for insubordination ... he accidentally came across a certain book and thought ... ah ... world ... could such a world exist? ... he was released but was still under surveillance ... he was captured when he tried to escape to the north ... I mention him because he also refused to change his political view ...

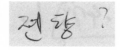

convert ?

change ?

view ?

. . . it was August . . . he was beaten severely . . . then his blood dried up . . . he was wearing a T-shirt under a uniform . . . he couldn't take them off till his scabs came off . . . he was all skin . . . he still refused to ? ? ? . . . then

물 고문

water torture

? ? ?

C N C

N V H

V R N

R T G

T ? ?

C H V

H N W

N G ?

G ?

... that didn't work either, so the guards tied him up to beat him ... I endured water torture twice ... I still didn't budge ... in winter the guards opened all the windows and doors of my cell and sprayed water ... I was stripped .... the cell turned into a freezer ... I could endure the cold for 6 days ... I squatted ... jumped to keep warm ... I was exhausted in the morning ... without food ... on day 7 I leaned against the ice wall and passed out ... I heard a siren ...

then I heard the vowels from my own mouth
O E
A E
I E
E E E
이 이 이

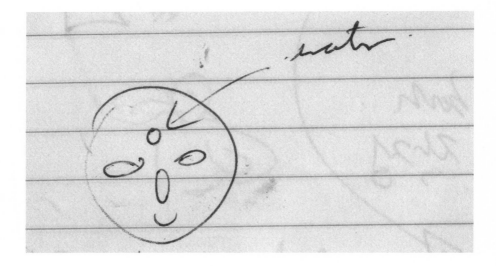

my face

browless

earless

my eyes

my nose

my mouth

moonless

my comet

. . . the guards aimed a jet of cold water at my forehead . . . full force . . . it looks like nothing

yet . . . it felt as if my head was being bashed with a rock . . . my toenails fell off . . . they kept

hitting my toes . . . unbearable pain . . . my toenails fell off . . . twice . . .

a siren

full speed

full orbit

full matter

full toenails

then I heard my vowels

oe

ae

ie

e

e

e

it looks like nothing yet

planets appeared in the sky

○] Mercury

○] Venus

○] Earth

○] Mars

○] Jupiter

○] Saturn

○] Uranus

○] Neptune

○] Pluto

○] Planet Nine

# Ahn Hak-sŏp #5

. . . the guards still used the Japanese word

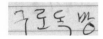

. . . a dark cell

. . . no blankets

. . . stripped naked

. . . I couldn't stretch my legs

. . . with a baton

. . . again and again

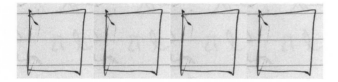

jab

butt

dig

poke

my square

my cosmos

my black hole

cornerless

. . . one guard asked me

. . . what if communism collapses all over the world?

. . . I said

. . . that has nothing to do with my ideology


. . . so a gang of thugs was sent in to terrorize me

. . . my head cracked


. . . I was on Planet Nine

. . . the torturer asked me

. . . what if I smash Planet Nine into bits?

. . . I said

. . . even blood rusts


. . . on Planet Nine

. . . snow was pink

. . . flakes of scabs

. . . dunes of dandruff


. . . the torturer asked

. . . what if I smash your head to bits?

. . . I said

. . . e e e

. . . ideology

# PLANETARY

# TRANSLATION

On December 15, 2016, I met Ahn-Kim Jeong-Ae—a feminist scholar and activist I knew through the International Women's Network Against Militarism—in a district called Insadong. I waited for her in a restaurant, watching and listening to a plain-clothes police officer talking on his phone as he slurped down his soup. Besides the usual busloads of young Korean soldiers (in compulsory military service) guarding the US embassy, downtown Seoul was crawling with police officers due to the weekly protest at Gwanghwamun Square. Citizens nationwide were demanding the impeachment of the corrupt president, Park Geun-hye, the daughter of former dictator Park Chung Hee.

From August 2005 to October 2007, during the progressive administration of President Roh Moo-hyun, Ahn-Kim had been involved in the investigation of abuses and human-rights violations committed by the South Korean military and its department of defense under the dictatorships of Park Chung Hee and his successor, Chun Doo Hwan. And from November 2007 to April 2010, as a lead researcher in the Truth and Reconciliation Commission of South Korea, Ahn-Kim investigated several cases concerning massacres of civilians that took place just before and during the Korean War.

For lunch, we ordered fresh oyster salad and bean-paste stew. Ahn-Kim began telling me about the cases she had researched. She jotted down on scratch paper names and places and mapped out for me unspeakable orbits of torture and atrocities.

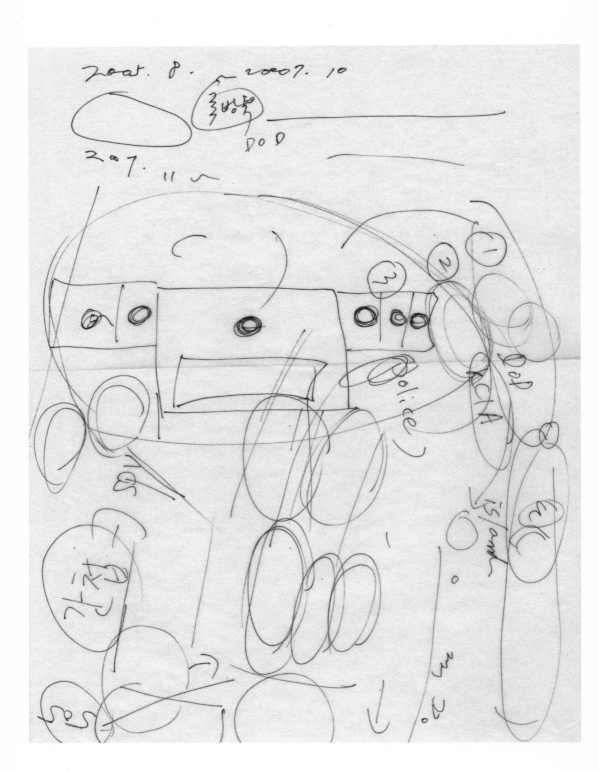

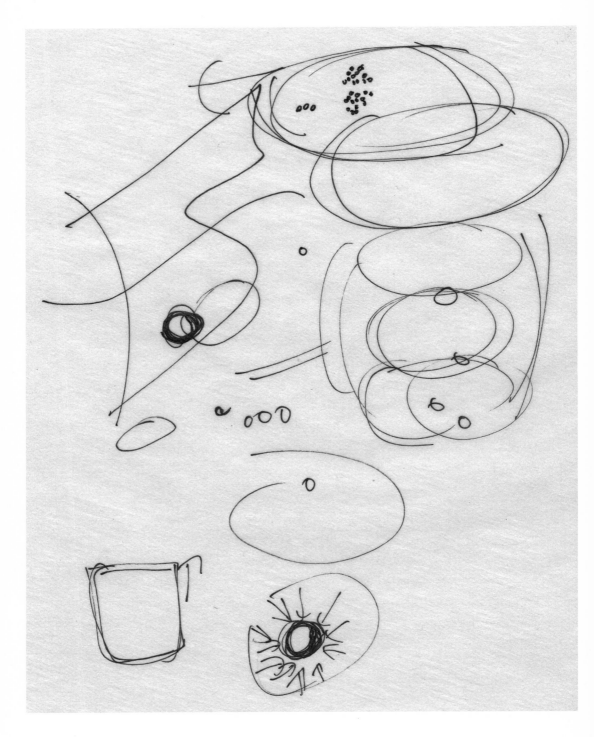

the end of a nation


------------------------------------------------------------Marfa, Texas

30.3095 north


On July 2, 2018, my flight took me to Marfa, Texas—not my usual migratory route. Nevertheless, during my brief stay, I was able to meet swallows and sparrows, and I observed other exceptional migratory wings from Mexico. Some small-winged children were captured and separated from their parents and placed in concentration camps along the border of Texas, US, and Mexico. Who will translate their wings? Whenever my ears would let me, I looked up at the night skies in order to track Planet Nine. Being the compulsive translator that I am, I traced and traced the planet's orbitary routes, its rotations of capture, torture, and massacre. The universe is such a dizzying place that my ears were spinning out of control. Planet Nine! Come in, Planet Nine!

The language of capture, torture, and massacre is difficult to decipher. It's practically a foreign language. What a nightmare! But as a foreigner myself, I am able to detect the slightest flicker of palpitations and pain. Difficult syntax! It may show up as faint dots and lines, but they're often blood, snow, and even dandruff. How do I know? Foreigners know. Ahn-Kim calmly narrated as she continued to circle and circle Planet Nine with her pen. Her circles were extraordinary.

# THE

# ORPHANS

**Édouard Glissant:**

*No imagination helps avert destitution in reality, none can oppose oppressions or sustain those who "withstand" in body or spirit. But imagination changes mentalities, however slowly it may go about this.*

trans. by Betsy Wing
from *Poetics of Relation*

One starless night, I was stranded. Needless to say, foreigners are often stranded. I decided to translate the stories of eight girls who survived the Sancheong-Hamyang massacre, which took place in Gyeongsangnam-do, a southern province of South Korea, in 1951. My decision to translate the girls' stories wasn't entirely mine alone. It can take billions of years for light to reach us through the galaxies, which is to say, History is ever arriving. So it's most likely that the decision, seemingly all mine, was already made years ago by someone else, which is to say, language—that is to say, translation—always arises from collective consciousness. Be factual, you say? As I mentioned, foreigners simply know. I will name the surviving orphans one by one in honor of the nameless children who are still homesick, captive, in detention, in internment, in concentration camps, in seas, in deserts, on Planet Nine, and such. And let's not forget the children who are still in school.

# Orphan Cheo Geum-jeom

## (age 13)

설이다. 아이 좋아라. 떡 많이 먹어 배가 부르다. 내가
제일 좋아하는 떡은 밤들어있는 송편이다. 손가락이 떨어질듯
추웠다. 그래도 친구집에 놀러 갔었다. 따발총 소리가 들리고
새카맣게 군인들이 몰려오는걸 보았다. 개미 같이 보였다. 그 것게
눈이 왔기 때문이다. 다들 나와! 하고 소리 지른다. 솜곱장난에
빠져있었다. 여름이라 동백꽃 잎4귀를 말아 아주 잘게 썰어서
국수 만들고 있었다. 아이 맛있어. 다 죽일거야! 하는데도 우린
정신 없이 놀았다. 마을 사람들 다 모아 놓았다. 한번도 엄마
우는걸 못 보았는데 엄마는 울고 있었다. 그래서 그런지 나도
저절로 따라 울었다. 군인들이 우리 마을 사람들 다 산으로 몰고
갔다. 엄마랑 밤 줍던 산속이다. 놀라는 바람에 신발이
벗겨진 것도 몰랐다. 그래서 더 울었다. 신발 없이 사는게
세상에서 재일 싫어서. 엄마 손 꼭 잡고 돌아섰다. 군인 들이
그러라 해서. 큰 구덩이 안을 들여다 보았다. 아무것도 보이지
않았다. 내 신발 어떻게 찾지 생각하고 있었는데 갑자기
엄마가 붕 떠올랐다 자꾸만 붕 떠올랐다. 나도 모르게
엄마 밑에 깔려있었다. 왼발에 모가 뚫고 들어갔다.
너무나 조용해 내 머리 안에 있는 노리들이 온 세상에 톡 들렸다.
갑자기 이번엔 내가 뛰어 서 있었다. 시신들이 불타고 있어서
너무 뜨거워서. 엄마 보니 머리가 없었다. 무서워. 삼촌은
피 투성이. 개울 넘어서 산 올라가는데 군인들이 총 다시 쏘았다.

New Year's Day! I was stuffed from eating too many rice cakes. My favorites are the ones with chestnuts in the middle. It was so cold that my fingers were ready to snap off, but I still went over to my friend's house to play. Then I heard a machine gun and saw a swarm of soldiers. They looked like ants against the snow. Come out! they shouted. We will kill you all! But my friend and I kept on playing. We pretended it was summer and made green noodles by rolling up camellia leaves and slicing them ever so thinly. Now all the village people were rounded up. My mom was crying, and I had never seen her cry before. Maybe that's why I started crying too. The soldiers made us go up the hill into the forest where my mom and I picked chestnuts. I was in such a panic that I didn't realize my shoes had come off. I cried even more. I hate being shoeless more than anything in the world. I held onto my mom's hand and turned around because the soldiers told us to. I looked down at the pit. I couldn't see anything but dirt. I thought to myself, How will I ever find my shoes again? Then suddenly my mom floated up in the air again and again. Somehow I was already lying beneath her. Somehow a bullet pierced through my left foot. Somehow it was so quiet that I could hear everything inside my head. Somehow I jumped up. All the corpses were burning. Somehow my mom was headless. My uncle, covered in blood, acted crazy. Somehow somehow. We ran across the creek and up the mountain. The soldiers saw us and started shooting again.

# Orphan Heo Jeom-dal

## (age 10)

저는 아직도 오줌싸기입니다. 똥간에 가는 게 무섭습니다. 엄마가 그러는데 머리에 키 쓰고 동네 집마다 가서 소금 받아 오게 한다고 항상 꾸지람 받습니다. 어느날 새벽에 군인들이 나타나서 나오라고 했습니다. 기저귀 찬 할머니 까지도 나와야 한다고 했습니다. 할아버진 추워서 누비옷 가지러 들어가려고 하니까 군인들이 막았습니다. 우리 집에 불을 질렀습니다. 억새로 지붕을 엮었기 때문에 불이 잘 붙었습니다. 군인들이 우리 식구 마을 사람들 골짜기에 떨어뜨려 놓고 총 쐈습니다. 그다음엔 시체에 불을 붙였습니다. 고기 굽는 냄새가 나 마구 토했습니다. 여동생은 총 7군데 맞아도 살아 있었습니다. 저는 총알이 왼쪽 뺨으로 뚫고 갔습니다. 웃지도 못합니다. 얼굴이 못하게 그럽니다. 불탄 방에서 동생을 간호했습니다. 그냥 쳐다만 보는 게 간호였습니다. 일주일 지나 군인들이 다시 돌아와 나가라고 해서 도망 가는데 동생은 꼼짝 못해 총에 맞아 다시 한번 죽었습니다. 아버지는 고모네 집에서 돌아가셨고요. 피 하나 안 흘리시고 물만 줄줄 흘리시다가 돌아가셨습니다. 세월이 지나니 꿈에서 엄마랑 동생이 보였습니다.

I still wet my bed. I was afraid to go to the outhouse. Mommy said she'd send me out with a winnowing shovel over my head and make me go from house to house and beg for salt. Soldiers appeared from nowhere and told us to come out, even my grandma in diapers. My grandpa wanted to go back into the house to get his quilted jacket but the soldiers stopped him. They set fire to our house. It burned fast because the roof was made of straw. The soldiers herded us into a ravine and shot us. Then they set the corpses on fire. The dead smelled like grilled meat, so I vomited. My sister was still alive after being shot seven times. As for me, a bullet went through my left cheek. I can't smile. My face won't let me. I nursed my sister in our burnt house. I just stared at the bullet holes on her body from morning till night. After a week the soldiers came back, and we fled. My sister couldn't move at all, so she was shot again. She died the second time. My father died at our aunt's house. He didn't bleed at all. But water kept streaming out from his wound. It was as deep as the ravine. Months later I saw Mommy and my sister in a dream. Water. I couldn't stop the water.

# Orphan Kim Gyeong-nam

## (age 16)

남동생이 피범벅이 되어 맨발로 집으로 돌아왔다
무덤에서 살아 나왔다.
동생이 죽은 사람들 밟고 왔다고 했다.
무덤에 피가 차올랐다고 했다.
내가 어머니 아버지가 자식들 버리고 도망 가드냐 했더니
남동생이 어머니 아버지 다 죽었다!
동생이 고래고래 소리 질렀다.
난 믿지 못했다.
아니다 어머니 아버지 살아 올기다.
우리 언니가 동생 살리라고 자기 치마 안으로 넣어
깔고 앉았다고 한다.
동생은 자꾸 고래고래 소리 질렀다
어머니 머리 탄 웅덩이 밖에 못 찾았다고
불도 끌 수도 없었다고
고래 고래 소리 질렀다.

My little brother came home barefoot covered in blood.

He got out alive from the mass grave.

He said, I stepped on dead bodies.

The grave filled with blood.

I asked, Did our parents run away without us?

No they are all dead.

He screamed and screamed.

I didn't believe him.

No they'll come back alive.

Our big sister hid my brother under her skirt and sat on him to keep him alive.

He screamed and screamed.

I could only grab a clump of Mother's hair.

I couldn't put out the flames.

Father sizzled and crackled.

My brother screamed and screamed.

In a dream I chew and chew Mother's hair.

# Orphan Kim Gap-sun

## (age 8)

빨갱이 할머니
빨갱이 할아버지
빨갱이 논두렁
빨갱이 엄마
빨갱이 치마
빨갱이 아버지
빨갱이 낫
빨갱이 언니
빨갱이 동생
빨갱이 오빠
빨갱이 조카
빨갱이 아기
빨갱이 친구
우리 다 반동새끼
엄마
빨갱이

commie grandma

commie grandpa

commie rice paddy

commie mother

commie skirt

commie father

commie sickle

commie sisters

commie brothers

commie nieces

commie nephews

commie baby

commie friend

we are all commie bastards

# Orphan Jeong Jeong-ja

## (age 8)

꿈에서 이모보고 달 만질수 있어 했어. 나만 빼놓고
다들 예쁜 저고리 치마 입었어. 엄마랑 언니는
나 버리고 어디 갔어. 눈이 왔어. 벼룩이 우글우글했어.
군인들이 있어 나와! 하고 소리 질렀어. 연설들어!
난 연설이 뭔지 몰랐어. 연설이 무서웠어. 빨갱이!
새끼들! 인간도 아니야! 개만큼도 못한 것들!
벼룩들이 어기저기 뛰면서 우리한테 침을 막
배 텄어. 퉤! 퉤! 연설이 무서웠어. 나만
울고불고 있었어. 그런데 배가 고팠어. 이모한테
은하수 만질 수 있어 했어.

In a dream I asked my auntie if I could touch the moon. Everyone was wearing pretty blouses and skirts except for me. My mom and sister took off, leaving me behind. It was snowing. I saw a cluster of fleas. They were soldiers. They yelled, Come out! Listen to our speech! I didn't know what speech was. Speech was scary. Commies! Bastards! Not even human! Not better than dogs! The fleas scattered, then began spitting at us. Rat-a-tat-tat! Rat-a-tat-tat! Speech was scary. I was the only one wailing in my dream. Then I was hungry. I asked my auntie if I could touch the Milky Way.

# Orphan Yu Gi-myo

## (age 13)

다리 절면서 식구 찾으러 논밭으로 나갔다. 어머니는 죽어있고 엎혀 있던
동생은 살아 있었다. 띠를 풀어서 동생을 업었다. 동생이 울고 있었는지
아닌지 기억이 안 난다. 따발총 소리에 귀가 멍해졌다. 군인들이
다시 돌아오고 있었다. 죽은 척했다. 어머니 배 위에 누웠다.
어머니 입이 벌려져 있었는데 점심때 국수 말아 먹은 냄새가
났다. 국수 한 가락이 어머니 목에 붙어 있다. 신음하는 소리가
나드니 누가 나 죽어라 했다. 군인들이 다시 총을 쏘았다. 논두렁
이에서 나오니 마을 사람들이 니 동생 다리 봐라 했다.
돌아보니 다리가 다 날아 가고 없었다. 똥 묻은 바지만 몸뚱이에
달려있었다. 반쯤 타버린 집에 들어가니 마을 사람들이 쉬고
있었다. 마을 사람들이 니 등에 살점 덩어리 붙어 있다 했다.
귀머거리 척했다. 끝. 고아 유기묘

I limped out to the rice paddy to look for my family. Mother was dead but my baby brother on her back was still alive. He'd shat his pants. I untied him and wrapped him around my back. I don't remember whether he was crying or not. My ears went numb after the machine guns went off. The soldiers came back to check. I pretended I was dead. I was on top of Mother's stomach. From her open mouth I could still smell the noodle soup she had for lunch. A strand of noodle around her neck looked like a neck-lace. Someone moaned and said, Finish me off. So the soldiers started shooting again. When I came out of the trench, village people said, Look at your brother's legs! I glanced over my shoulder. His legs were gone. I could only see his soiled, tattered pants. When I arrived home, village people were huddled inside because their houses had burned down. They said, Look at the lump of flesh stuck to your back! I pretended I was deaf. The end.

# Orphan Yi Jeong-seon

## (age 7)

연설이 계속 시끄러웠는데 뒷간에 가야 했어.

그런데 엄마는 가지 말라고 했어. 작은 구멍 파서

누우라고 했어. 뻥 하고 터졌어! 난 기절했어.

눈 뜨니까 구덩이 안이 깜깜했어. 팔 없고

다리 없고 머리도 없는 사람들 만지며

엄마 찾았어. 내 머리가 빙빙 돌아갔어.

엄마가 흰 옷 입고 머리 풀고 우리 집 반대 쪽으로

가는걸 봤어. 따라갔어. 칠성은 나 따라오고. 은하수

도 넘어갔어. 그런데 엄마가 아니라 귀신이었어. 그래서

돌아서서 걸어갔어. 집에 언니가 와 있었어.

매일 울었어. 학교도 못 갔어 밥도 못 먹었어.

깨죽만 먹고 살았어.

I had to go to the outhouse while the speech was still loud, but Mommy told me to stay put. She dug me a little hole and told me to lie in it. Then—boom! I fainted. When I opened my eyes it was dark inside the hole. I touched armless, legless, headless bodies, looking for Mommy. My head spun countless times. I saw Mommy all in white with her hair down walking away from our house. I followed her. And the Big Dipper followed me. I even crossed the Milky Way. What I saw was a ghost, so I turned around and walked back. My sister was already home. I wept every day. I couldn't go to school. I couldn't eat. I lived on sesame porridge for a year.

# Orphan Kim Seong-rye

## (age 15)

수많은 시커멓게 된 시신들을 봤습니다. 시체가 즐비한 것도 봤습니다.

다음 해 비 오는 날 구덩이에서 우는 소리가 들렸습니다.

숲속에 인불이 날아다니는 것도 보았습니다.

인불이 날 빙빙 돌았습니다.

I saw countless charred bodies. I saw rows and rows of corpses.

A year later on a rainy summer day I heard cries from the pit. Oblong oblong.

I saw ghosts floating about in the forest. They circled and circled me.

# Orphan Nine

I went on a tour of Ilya Kabakov's *School No. 6.* It's an imaginary school, abandoned in the desert just like an orphan. One famous critic said that the schoolhouse and children represent the future, a utopia! No, this is not speech. I may be the only one who thinks this but representation can be magical. Cruelty and beauty — how do they coexist? I wish the eight orphans could have attended this school. They could have shown the Russian children how to make green noodles from camellia leaves. And the Russian children could have read to them their favorite fairy tale, "Snow White." The guide told us that a big snake lives alone in the school courtyard among over-grown grass and dead trees no birds will perch on. What a void! But the music room was enchanting. There were many stories written by schoolchildren. They wrote about their class events, how they repaired their school, how they behaved on a trip to the museum, and so on. Their notebooks strewn on the dusty wooden floors were not that different from mine — "discarded notebooks that no one needs," according to the artist. I wish the orphan girls could have written their school stories too. I was thinking that the floors could use a good rubbing with sesame oil, the way children polished the floors at my old school, when I noticed a faded butterfly postcard on the floor. Another card next to it had pink roses. How perfect! The artist had thought of everything, as a child does. The roses looked like camellia blossoms, so I made a quick sketch for my mother. My mother always looked for camellia blossoms in our flight. I wish the orphan girls could have sketched the roses for their mothers too. I didn't know Snow White also flew with snow geese. But that's what the artist painted, pre-tending to be one of the schoolchildren: Illustration for the fairy tale by Ostrovsky, "Snow White." In fact, he pretends to be all the children at the imaginary school while I pretend to be deaf. I may be the only one who thinks this, but his translation of "The

Snow Maiden" as "Snow White" is sublime. As I said, representation can be magical. Anyway, Snow White is displayed in the glass case of the school announcement board. I wish paintings of orphan girls could be on display, too, behind the glass. Then they could live forever inside a utopia! I wish and wish! It looks as if Snow White can touch the Milky Way! I wish and wish!

БЕРЕГИТЕ
КНИГУ-
ИСТОЧНИК
ЗНАНИЯ!

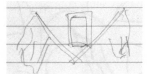

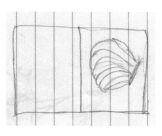

Who am I?

You are Halo

Who am I?

You are Oblong

Who am I?

You are Snow

Who am I?

You are Snow Pink

# THE

# APPARATUS

**IN THE PENAL COLONY:** "It's a remarkable piece of apparatus" however "the explorer did not much care about the apparatus" and noted "These uniforms are too heavy for the tropics, surely" nonetheless "the officer" said "but they mean home to us; we don't want to forget about home" however "the officer" phonated "Have you ever heard of our former Commandant?" still "A pity you never met the old Commandant!" anyhow lingually "here stands his apparatus before us" and withal "The lower one is called the 'Bed,' the upper one the 'Designer,' and this one here in the middle that moves up and down is called the 'Harrow'" after all "the officer was speaking French" though utterly "neither the soldier nor the prisoner understood a word of French" even so "the explorer" noted again "It was all the more remarkable, therefore, that the prisoner was nonetheless making an effort to follow the officer's explanations" yet verbally "The Bed and the Designer were of the same size."

**IN THE NEOCOLONY:** "Horrific!" "(the translator who made herself as lowly as she could)" reuttered in Korean "discarded language that no one needs, surely" however "the investigator" in turn added phonetically "The US military!" "[The neocolonizer!]" yet "the prisoner said he understood Japanese" noted "(the translator who didn't know a word of it, and was equally foreign to English—hence lowly)" regardless "(the investigator)" sonated "The Japanese military!" "[The former colonizer!]" and recounted "The military apparatus" "The intelligence apparatus" "The police apparatus" even so "What? Precisely this: that the upper floors could not 'stay up' (in the air) alone, if they did not rest precisely on their base" "(Althusser)" but then "(the translator)" politely paraphrased in translation "there was no Bed to begin with" "soldiers who didn't know a word of English" "only had to use their innate muscles to dig deeper holes and trenches" "a primitive apparatus, surely" "commies, surely" then rattled on "while the US military apparatus provided extra manpower, machine guns, and essential trucks to transport the commies to their rightful digs" "Rat-a-tat-tat!" "Rat-a-tat-tat!" In other words "[commie genocide]." And "[before the war the US-backed commandant, Syngman Rhee, kept a list of 300,000 commies in order to eradicate them]"—"[of course we couldn't count every single civilian who was killed]"—"[some were chained to rocks and drowned in the sea]"—"[the so-called commies were mostly farmers, elders, women, children who lived in villages beneath so-called commie mountains where the anti-colonial guerrilla fighters hid during the day and came down at night to collect provisions]" "(the investigator)" patiently spelled out as she kept drawing "extraordinary circles" while "(the translator)" could only helplessly flutter her ears. Anyhow, "The State apparatus, which defines the State as a force of repressive execution and intervention 'in the interests of the ruling classes [and the neocolonizer]' in the class struggle conducted by the bourgeoisie and its allies against the proletariat [the neocolonized], is quite certainly the State, and quite certainly defines its basic 'function'" enunciated "(Althusser)."

**IN THE PENAL COLONY:**   "Does he know his sentence?" "(the explorer)"

"No" "(the officer)"

"He doesn't know the sentence that has been passed on him?" "(the explorer)"

"No" "(the officer)"

"There would be no point in telling him. He'll learn it on his body" "(the officer)"

"Whatever commandment the prisoner has disobeyed is written upon his body by the Harrow" "(the officer)"

"HONOR THY SUPERIORS!" "(the Harrow)"

**IN THE NEOCOLONY:**   (HONOR THY SKY!) "the old wisdom"

(YOU EVIL BITCHES!) "the neocolonial wisdom"

(HONOR THY KING!) "the old wisdom"

(YOU SCUMS OF SOCIETY!) "the neocolonial wis-dom"

(HONOR THY HUSBAND!) "the old wisdom"

(YOU!) "the neocolonial wisdom"

(HONOR THY SON!) "the old wisdom"

(Before the woman was released, that is to say, after she was clubbed nonstop for an entire month, she received orders to bathe at a creek in a remote area. When she took off her clothes, the same ones she was wearing the day she was captured for no apparent reason and put into a so-called "mind-heart-soul" reform camp under the command of a new commandant [one more US-backed dictator, a.k.a. "Your Excellency"] [for there is never a shortage of them]—after all the police had to fill a certain quota of women [300 out of 60,000]—the woman went into shock from what she saw. Her whole body was blue! There wasn't a single part of her body that was not blue from the savage beatings. She thought she was the only blue one, but the woman next to her was also blue! The woman in front of her was, again, blue! And the woman behind her was totally blue!) "the investigator"

(BLUE × 300!) "the translator"

**IN THE PENAL COLONY:** (The batons energized by muscles alone lack the technology and sophistication of the Harrow but nonetheless they should be understood as instruments of writing) "the translator"

(Are you saying blue can be translated?) "the USA"

(Yes, blue can be translated as "BLUE × 300," without the exclamation mark, if need be) "the translator"

("LOST IN TRANSLATION" is an old wisdom) "the translator"

("TRANSLATOR, TRAITOR" rhymes yet is undoubtedly an old wisdom) "the translator"

("WE DON'T WANT TO FORGET ABOUT HOME" is entirely universal and therefore remains untranslatable) "the translator" [who was terribly homesick even at home—the translator is without a uniform, mind you]

("In order to advance the theory of the [neocolonial] State) (I shall call this reality by its concept: *the* [neocolonial] *Ideological State Apparatuses*") "Althusser"

(And in order to advance the theory of translation I translate "the State" as "the [neocolonial] State" and *"the Ideological State Apparatuses"* as *"the* [neocolonial] *Ideological State Apparatuses"* and "the USA" as "the united status of apparatus" considering ample "reality" has already been offered to the curious reader [not to dismiss "the USAs"] [plurality of reality propels translation] [difference propels theory] [memory propels art] [which may all be beside the point]) "the translator"

("But now for what is essential. What distinguishes the ISAs from the (Repressive) State Apparatus is the following basic difference: the Repressive State Apparatus functions 'by violence,' whereas the Ideological State Apparatuses *function 'by ideology'* ") "Althusser"

**IN THE NEOCOLONY:**  "(. . .)" "(e e e)" "(. . .)" "(ideology)" "(. . .)" (Mr. Ahn)

"(ideology)" "(ideology is the system of the ideas and representations which dominate the mind of a man or a social group)" "(ideology)" "(before Freud)" "(is for Marx an imaginary assemblage)" "(*bricolage*)" "(a pure dream, empty and vain)" "('day's residues')" "(It is on this basis)" "(ideology)" "(has no history)" "(since its history is outside it)" "(ideology)" "(can and must)" "(be related directly to)" "(Freud's proposition)" "(that *the unconscious is eternal*)" "(i.e. that it has no history)" "(if)" "(eternal)" "(means)" "(not transcendent)" "(but)" "(omnipresent)" "(trans-historical)" "(and therefore)" "(I shall adopt Freud's expression)" "(word for word)" "(and write)" "(*ideology is eternal*)" "(exactly)" "(like)" "(the unconscious)" "(the eternity of the unconscious)" "(is not)" "(unrelated)" "(to the)" "(eternity of ideology)" "(in general)" (Althusser)

**IN THE NEOCOLONY:** "(. . .)" "(e e e)" "(. . .)" "(I was on Planet e)" "(. . .)" (Mr. Ahn)

"(Ideology has a material existence)" "(ideology)" "(always exists in an apparatus)" "(ideology)" "(=)" "(an imaginary relation to real relations)" "(imaginary relation)" "(is)" "(itself endowed with a material existence)" (Althusser)

(e e e) (=) (ideology) (=) (imaginary) (=) (eternity) (the translator)

**IN THE NEOCOLONY:** (eliminate) (eradicate) (obliterate) (the National Security Law apparatus)

(will you change your political view or not?) (old Your Excellency)

(will you change your political view or not?) (new Your Excellency)

"(oe)" "(ae)" "(ie)" "(e)" "(e)" "(e)" (Mr. Ahn)

**IN THE PENAL COLONY:** 10. Have you EVER been a member of, or in any way associated with the Communist Party? (old INS apparatus)

10. Have you EVER been a member of, or in any way associated (either directly or indirectly) with: A. The Communist Party? B. Any other totalitarian party? C. A terrorist organization? (new USCIS apparatus)

(chorus of allegiance: E V E R , E V E R , E V E R )

A. Eternity

B. Eternity

C. Eternity

**IN THE DMZ COLONY:**    I'll leave it up to your imagination

A. 이

B. 이

C. 이

# INTERPELLATION

## OF

## RETURN

**Louis Althusser:**

*I shall then suggest that ideology "acts" or "functions" in such a way that it "recruits" subjects among the individuals (it recruits them all), or "transforms" the individuals into subjects (it transforms them all) by that very precise operation which I have called* interpellation *or hailing, and which can be imagined along the lines of the most commonplace everyday police (or other) hailing: "Hey, you there!"*

trans. by Ben Brewster

from *Lenin and Philosophy and Other Essays*

더러 避亂하러 갔으로 獨立郡으로 ─ 午參

十時頃에 鰊林 西쪽 土防에 設置한 五...人間에 ... 退

들오 皇子 先納 ... 通身 ... 롯 수力子

들을 또 ... 自身이 또連人 ... 于... 名이

러니서 老人 ... 來城年에 ... 陳外서 ...名이

몸을 西洲里 南쪽 山下에 ... 또 ...

구둥이다 ... 코 手 揄彈 ... 被傷 ... 連繫

難하야 被傷 ... ... 良民으로 ...處

유식

四山情神 生草面 ... 以下 ... 病患 四 ... 二月 ... 午后 七時頃

上端洞 生草面 ... 西 民學校

ㄴ. 如故龍 第九聯隊 第三大隊

ㄷ. 裸虫地况

第一敎室再 따루二個所

第五敎室內 따루一個所

(2) 多枚丹咨

第九聯隊水行達中月敎에서 外遠達

最携荷子筆을燒却않고마는敎출을逃

(3) 週일狀况

第九聯隊車三大隊人員이千名이什罕進中

同彼에이끼가水(枕休態하케되났는데

으로煩燥에가살을되몸눈더大急不遠二도살노量豈乐

머러저第一敎室及第五敎室內마는에直狸이千

These two pages are from the 1951 record of the Counterintelligence Corps of South Korea, regarding the Sancheong-Hamyang massacre. A total of 705 were killed, among them 147 children under 14 years of age, 189 men, and 197 women. Only 386 have been officially identified. Until recently, the Sancheong-Hamyang massacre was lumped together with the more widely known Geochang massacre. According to Ahn-Kim, such nondifferentiation or reduction is how the state continues to suppress knowledge regarding the mass executions of civilians that took place before and during the war. Through concealment, through falsification, through control, through "hailing": "Hey, you there!" "Commies." "YOU." The Sancheong-Hamyang-Geochang massacres, which led to 1,424 deaths, were carried out by the soldiers of the 11th ROK Army from February 4, 1951, to February 11, 1951, under the command of Syngman Rhee, one of the main "cogwheels" of "the Designer."

In April 1960, my father photographed and filmed the student-led revolution, referred to as the April 19 Student Revolution, that toppled Syngman Rhee's administration. Rhee escaped to Hawaii and died in 1965. Escape and exile must be differentiated. The cogwheels are often given the privilege of escape because "the Designer," too, thinks of everything. (It was noted earlier that children and artists think of everything. Unlike "the Designer," they think outside of interpellation, which is to say, they think of snow, which is to say, they think of everything in order to resist as subjects.) The victims of History are permanently exiled from home, within and without. The practitioners of memory are also. We live as foreigners, as translators. We translate everything, including what "the Harrow" has written. We see the point of rescribing everything written upon the bodies.

Before the Korean War, under Rhee's dictatorship, 300,000 so-called communists and suspected sympathizers were forcibly enrolled into Bodo League, a "re-education" league. It was a mechanism of surveillance, then later a mechanism of genocide—"the Bed." It is estimated that 100,000 to 200,000 were killed during the single month of June in 1950, the same month the war began. Koreans indiscriminately killing Koreans. How does this happen? The Koreans, already colonized by the Japanese military machine, were ready-made to be neocolonized by the US military machine. Not difficult to see each other as "scums of society," "commies." After all, (America) (=) (Beauty) (=) (Me=Gook). All we needed was language. All we needed was eternity. Many victims of Sancheong, Hamyang, and Geochang were found to have enlisted in the re-education league, that is to say, the commandment they had disobeyed was written upon their bodies, that is to say, they learned their sentence on their bodies.

As Ahn-Kim told me, it was not possible for her investigative team to count everyone who had perished. It is not possible to count ideology. It is not possible to count e. It is not possible to count snow. It is not possible to count blue. They are all eternal. They are "the eternity of the unconscious." They can only be recounted through memory, through "an imaginary assemblage," "*bricolage*," through the "hailing" of return.

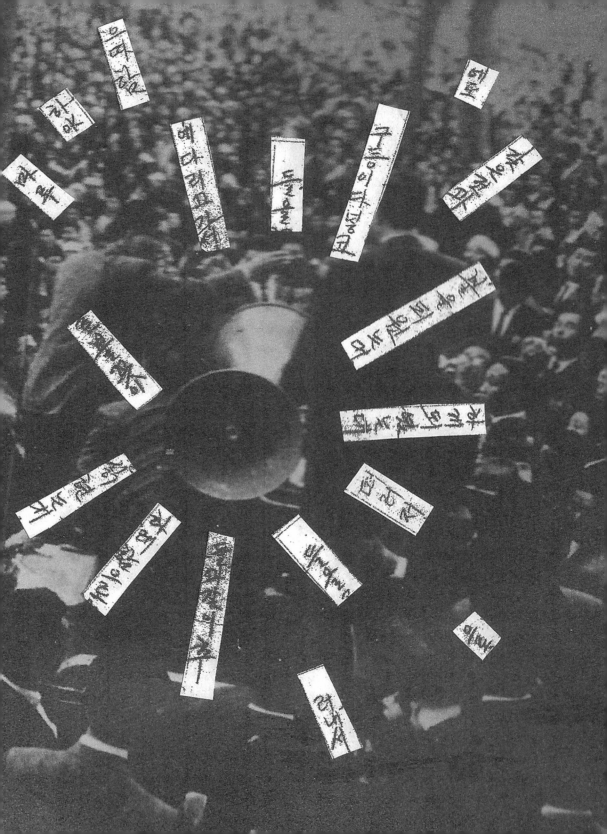

# MIRROR

# WORDS

**Gilles Deleuze and Félix Guattari:**

*Language is made not to be believed but to be obeyed, and to compel obedience.*

trans. by Brian Massumi

from *A Thousand Plateaus*


**Gilles Deleuze:**

*Information is a controlled system of order words. Order words that are given in our society.*

trans. by Alison M. Gingeras

from "What Is the Creative Act?"


**Kim Hyesoon:**

*It may be that women's or death's song is sung only in vowels, without the consonants.*

trans. by Don Mee Choi

from *Autobiography of Death*

Mirror words come out of my thoughts about translation: Translation is a mode=
Translation is an anti-neocolonial mode. I obsess about "order words that are given
in our society." In 1945, it took less than thirty minutes for order words to be carried
out, to divide the country I was born in, along the 38th parallel north. Order words
compel division, war, and obedience around the world. But other words are possible.
Translation as an anti-neocolonial mode can create other words. I call mine mirror
words. Mirror words are meant to compel disobedience, resistance. Mirror words
defy neocolonial borders, blockades. Mirror words flutter along borders and are often
in flight across oceans, even galaxies. Mirror words are homesick. Mirror words are
halo. Mirror words are orphaned words. Now look at your words in a mirror. Trans-
late, translate! Did you? Do it again, do it!

Ruoy Ycnellecxe **,**

Si ti Laitram Wal?

## Laturb Eripme*!*

Ruoy slagelli **,** Ruoy seegufer **,** Ruoy laretalloc egamad fo eht dlrow

# Etinu tsniaga Ruoy raer **.**

Ew era evila **.**

*Noitalsnart si a edom*

*Toward Global Humanity*

*Noitalsnart si na itna-lainolocoen edom*

Who are you?

I am Snow

Who are you?

I am Mode

I am Mode

I speak as a twin

October 26, 1979

Your Excellency,

I present to you a correspondence of certain grave significance. It's written in a foreign language. No translators are currently available. The members of your cabinet may not have any tolerance for foreign words or incomprehensibility in general. And the photograph is of an event in the near past or future. Time is irrelevant, time is minuscule. However, you, Sir, may recognize many of the letters. Now I leave you to your own pleasure, in your room, alone, fully alive. *Edom, edom*, I repeat. *Edom.*

Yours faithfully,
*Gnihton ta Lla*

Ruoy Ycnellecxe, Si ti Laitram Wal?

Ro na elbattegrofnu nossel?

Ruoy Ycnellecxe, Erehw si Nuhc Ood-Nawh? Ruoy Ycnellecxe, Era uoy evila?

Si Nuhc evila?

*Laturb Noitan!* Era uoy evila?

ㄱ-ㅏ-ㄱ-ㅎ-ㅏ-ㄱ-ㅖ-ㅇ-ㅓ-ㅁ-ㄹ-ㅕ-ㅇ-ㅇ-ㅣ-ㅂ-ㄴ-
ㅣ-ㄲ-ㅏ

# Sky Similes for Snow Geese

| ㄱ | consonant | |
| ㅏ | vowel | return . . . black-faced spoonbill . . . return |
| ㄱ | consonant | |
| ㅎ | consonant | |
| ㅏ | vowel | return . . . red-crowned crane . . . return |
| ㄱ | consonant | |
| ㅖ | vowel | return . . . white-naped crane . . . return |
| ㅇ | consonant | |
| ㅓ | vowel | sparrow, what took you so long? |
| ㅁ | consonant | |
| ㄹ | consonant | |
| ㅕ | vowel | during the Korean War cranes had no place to land |
| ㅇ | consonant | |
| ㅇ | consonant | |
| ㅣ | vowel | north . . . south . . . north |
| ㅂ | consonant | |
| ㄴ | consonant | |
| ㅣ | vowel | dead . . . dead . . . dead |
| ㄲ | consonant | |
| ㅏ | vowel | sky . . . sky . . . sky |

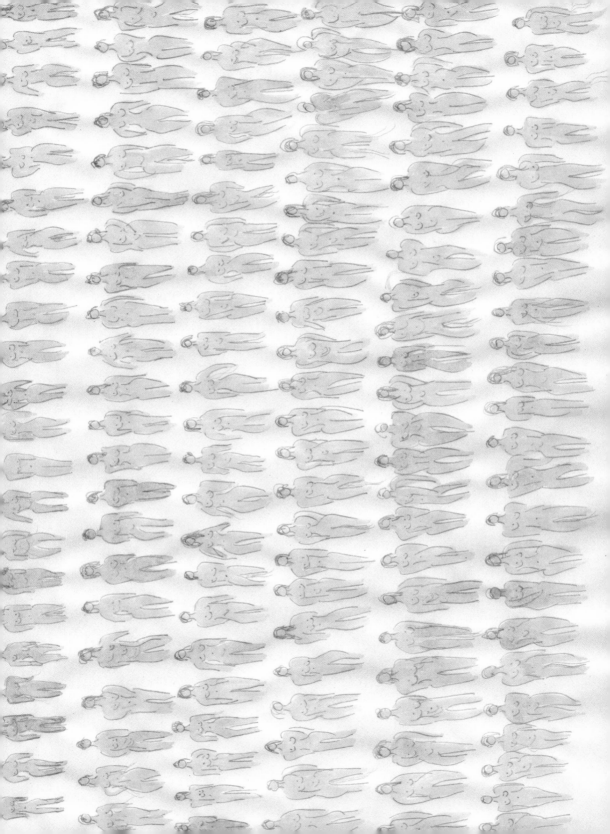

# (NEO)

# (=)

# (ANGELS)

**Frantz Fanon:**

*Because it is a systematic negation of the other person and a furious determination to deny the other person all attributes of humanity, colonialism forces the people it dominates to ask them-selves the question constantly: "In reality, who am I?"*

trans. by Constance Farrington
from *The Wretched of the Earth*


**Nagisa Oshima:**

*Yi Yunbogi, you are a 10-year-old boy.*

*Yi Yunbogi, you are a 10-year-old Korean boy.*

*Yi Yunbogi, you sell gum in the city.*

*Yi Yunbogi, you are one of them.*

*Yi Yunbogi, where is your mother?*

*Yi Yunbogi, don't blame your father.*

*Yi Yunbogi, you too were born during the Korean War.*

*An orphan who's not an orphan.*

from *Diary of Yunbogi* (film, 1965)

In reality, we were all angels. We were angels in white blouses like the white-naped cranes. Where are our mothers? We don't blame our fathers. They are wounded and ill. We too were born during the war, the year of the student revolution, after the coup, always during martial law. We are all orphans, orphans who aren't orphans. Angels who aren't angels. We too cried. We too sang, oblong oblong.

We too were born under the bridge. Every night, we listened to the whispers of the angels bathing in the river. They too cried and sang, Sky, sky, sky. Our lullaby. They didn't blame our nations. Migrating from pole to pole they watched our falling stars, our failing planet. They too were hungry. They too were homesick. We the feather-less watched the angels depart. Our farewell. In reality, we were all motherless.

We the angels who aren't angels stared into your photographs of the first republic of
South Korea. American generals. They too cried. They too sang. Freely in their lan-
guage. Our new fathers. We the orphans who aren't orphans cheered in our new
tongue and fluttered our wings of parade. In our language—suicide parade. Father,
where are you? But I was not born yet. Angels are never born, some say. Some say
wings sprout behind our ears.

In reality, who are you? Your birthday never certain, you asked, Who am I, really? Yet the birth of a division is certain and constant. Your photographs showed us. Each hand/ each grasp/ each angel. And I was born long after the masses of angels had cheered and wept in syncopation. Bombs too fell from the sky. I did what the snow geese do. I wrote in the sky—Return forever. We followed in the direction of Mother's pointed shoe. We landed. We took flight. We frayed. Our eyelids unfolded like Mother's umbrella.

Flowers on dresses/ flowers on mountains/ sparrows at DMZ/ red-crowned cranes feeding nearby/ spoonbills flying low/ *montage is an idea that arises from the collision of independent shots*/ a panorama of divided chirps/ a panorama of divided identity/ who am I, really?/ my mentor the flag eraser/ Paek Un-sŏn of *Dong-A Daily*/ scratched out the Japanese flag/ photo of the Korean marathon winner/ 1936 Berlin Olympics/ a shot of Japanese occupation/ a shot of American occupation/ not a collision of ideas at all/ a panorama of oblong/ a panorama of obelus/ umbrella forever/ vowels forever.

reality, we were all angels from DMZ. We too mingled, laughed, and played und
e skies of Panmunjom. Listen, angels, we are the orphans who aren't orphans. W
e the *obtuse/ the third meaning/ the passage from language/* to insignificance/
ernity/ to colony/ to colony. Halo to halo, hand to hand, we wave. Hello, ange

Dear angels, I speak to you today about the importance of nation, a nation that's not a nation. The American-backed angel of genocide has departed to Hawaii. Farewell forever. Now we must address our eternity. Our eternity of obelus! Our eternity of oblong! Our eternity of war! Are we orphans of beauty? Are we angels of eternity? Who are we, really?

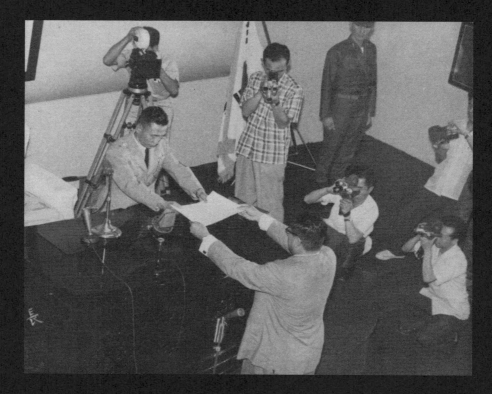

Your excellency, is it martial law? Is it of grave significance? Is it written in a foreign language? Your excellency, no translators are currently available. I squat beneath you. My film, *a signifier without a signified*. The American cabinet has no tolerance for foreign words. We the nameless. Who are you? We are the angels of America. Who are you? We are the angels of America. We bow to no one in particular.

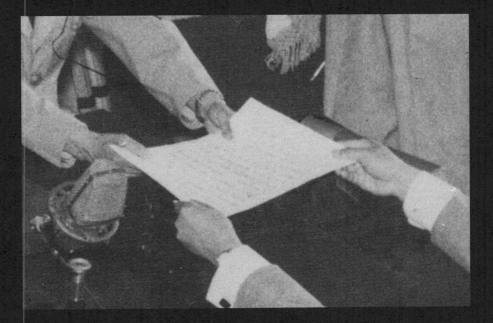

Our vowels are incomprehensible. Only the consonants pass from hand to hand, colony to colony. We cheer, we weep. We are e. We are 이. We are eternally motherless. We are your orphans. We are your angels. We are your mirror words. What's written on paper is obvious—See you at DMZ!

# Notes

"Sky Translation": I wrote the letters *D*, *M*, and *Z* on tracing paper over the photos I took of the skies when I heard the migrating snow geese.

"Wings of Return": In December 2016, I happened to walk into the old city hall in downtown Seoul. It is now a library for the city's archival documents. The entrance made me think about my father's story—how he had filmed the martial-law parade held in front of the hall and briefly encountered the former dictator, Park Chung Hee, who led the May 16, 1961, military coup with other generals. On the third floor, I wandered into the mayor's office. On the wall to my left was a display of the city's timeline with photos marking Seoul's major historical events. I spotted my father in the photo of the 1961 coup—the day of the martial-law declaration in front of the city hall. He is in the bottom left of the photo, holding his camera. The photo, taken by former AP photojournalist Kim Ch'ŏn-gil, is in the public domain of South Korea. In *Hardly War*, I used a very similar photo. I hid the faces of the generals with flowers. At that time, I didn't know the photo was taken by Kim. It turns out that my father and Kim knew each other very well. In their work as photojournalists, they often found themselves dispatched to the DMZ's Panmunjom, also known as the Truce Village, where meetings between North and South Korean officials took place. In my father's photo album, I found several photos in which he and Kim appear together. Kim passed away at age 89 in the US, in 2018. My father is still alive and lives with my mother at my older brother's house in Australia. In 1980, my father also gave KBS and MBC, South Korean broadcasters, copies of his news footage of the student protest in downtown Seoul.

"Ahn Hak-sŏp #1–5": I was introduced to Mr. Ahn by my friend, an artist and writer, Ahn Il Soon. Her father was a doctor, and during the Korean War he treated everyone, North and

South Korean, who needed medical attention. After the war, he was accused of being a North Korean sympathizer, so he was under constant surveillance and often interrogated and tortured. Because of this history, my friend Ahn Il Soon knew about Mr. Ahn and his struggles. Mr. Ahn and his wife kindly received me and my husband, Jay Weaver, into their home on December 23, 2016.

"Ahn Hak-sŏp #3": I jotted in Korean "태로," which is a transliteration of "terror." My messy handwriting enabled the first Korean consonant and vowel ㅌ and ㅐ to appear as if they were the English letters G and H, hence "GH로." 로 [ro] means "to/toward." And therefore, "Toward Global Humanity."

"Ahn Hak-sŏp #4": The clusters of consonants and question marks are from "convert ? / change ? / view ?" The clusters of vowels are also from the same words. I arranged the consonants and question marks like this—c n v r t? / c h n g ? / v w ?—in order to derive a series of possible clusters. The Korean word 이 sounds the same as the letter e/E. 이 is a homonym for this, teeth, lice, and two. And e is for ideology, empire, torture, and yet it has other possibilities such as Earth, Equality, Internationality, etc.

"Planetary Translation": I made the tracings from Ahn-Kim's scribbles on scratch paper. The Truth and Reconciliation Commission of South Korea had been discontinued during the two previous conservative administrations of Lee Myung-bak and Park Geun-hye. According to Ahn-Kim, many of the findings she uncovered on military, police, and Korean Intelligence had been classified for over thirty years, locked away in the Korean National Archives. Currently Ahn-Kim is active in South Korean women's and international women's organizations, including Women Making Peace and Women Cross DMZ.

"The Orphans": These imagined accounts are based on what Ahn-Kim told me when I met with her in 2016. She also gave me Sancheong-Hamyang Massacres of Civilians (2011), conference proceedings which contain findings and analysis by Ahn-Kim as well as transcribed oral testimonies of the survivors. The year 2011 was the 60th anniversary of the massacre. Thus, these imaginary stories are based on reality—history—yours and mine, and dreams—theirs and mine, and memory—theirs and mine. This is just another way of saying that "The Orphans" are poems, poetry of the unconscious. I first wrote them in Korean, then translated them. It made most sense to deploy my childish handwriting—it didn't have much of a chance to grow up outside of Korea. These poems in Korean and English are not exactly identical, as no translations are. It's just that there are always two of us—the eternal twoness.

"Orphan Nine": I am referring to Boris Groys's lecture "Kabakov as Illustrator," given on October 12, 2002, at the opening of Ilya Kabakov's exhibition *Children's Books and Related Drawings* at the Chinati Foundation in Marfa, Texas. "Discarded notebooks that no one needs" is from *Chinati: The Vision of Donald Judd* (2010). On July 15, 2018, Josh Jones, an artist who lives in Marfa and the tour guide for Chinati's full collection, allowed me extra time to view Kabakov's installation *School No. 6* so I could draw sketches of Kabakov's "Snow White." I drew the sketch of *School No. 6* outside the renovated artillery sheds that house Donald Judd's aluminum boxes, which I thought acted as mirror boxes (not unlike the mirrors used in telescopes at McDonald Observatory), gathering light from the past as well as diffusing it to the future. Judd's boxes were like language boxes filled with sounds only the children who pretended to be deaf could hear.

"The Apparatus": Some lines are from Franz Kafka's "In the Penal Colony," translated by Willa and Edwin Muir in *The Complete Stories* (Schocken Books, Inc., 1971); others are from Louis Althusser's "Ideology and Ideological State Apparatuses," translated by Ben Brewster in *Lenin and Philosophy and Other Essays* (Monthly Review Press, 2001). I was naturalized in the old Immigration and Naturalization Service (INS) building in Seattle. The second floor, with barred windows, was used for detaining the so-called undocumented. Sometimes the detainees shouted and waved. I was asked question number 10 about communism multiple times. I knew how to be consistent with my answers. Consistency not only applies to the rules of grammar, but also to the rules of border crossing and immigration. Consistency can signal legitimacy whether one is legitimate or not. But too much of it can raise a red flag. No pun intended. In the end, repetition became too tiresome for the officer. Ruffled feathers— mostly mine. I am one of those privileged ones. Number 10 and ○] are like twins, unbearably conjoined.

"Interpellation of Return": The photographs are my father's, of the April 19, 1960, Student Revolution in Seoul, South Korea.

"Mirror Words": The words written backwards were inspired by Ingmar Bergman's made-up language in his film *The Silence* (1963).

The "Toward Global Humanity" photo is my father's, of the student revolution. The blurred photo of twins is a close-up from the same photo.

The photo of a student about to be beaten with a baton is by the South Korean journalist Na Kyung-taek, from 518기 자 클 럽 , http://blog.naver.com/518photoclub. This site contains photos taken by Na during the May 18 Democratic Uprising in 1980, Gwangju, South Korea.

In "Sky Similes for Snow Geese," I separated out the Korean consonants and vowels sequentially. They make up the phrase: "Your excellency, is it martial law?"

"(Blue × 300!)": Pencil and watercolor on vellum paper.

"(Neo) (=) (Angels)": The photos are my father's, some were taken by his colleagues and given to him as keepsakes. My father talked to me about these photos in his album when I visited him in 2016. His ability to remember the details of time, light, and space never fails to astound me. As a child of memory, I have no choice but to continue my pursuit of memory, memory against history, the history of oblivion.

The shots in "(Neo) (=) (Angels)," in order of appearance:

- My sister and me in Seoul. My sister once told me over the phone, "We are all angels!" (page 115)

- Hangang Bridge, rebuilt after the war. I grew up next to the bridge. (page 116)

- My father's photos of the August 15, 1948, inauguration of the South Korean government on display in Seoul. (page 117)

- A close-up/ my father as a toddler/ my mother soon after she married my father. My father told me that he has always questioned his identity partly because he has never been certain about his date of birth. In his generation, parents took their time to add their children's names to the family registry. It was common in my father's generation for infants not to survive the first twelve months. In his family, nobody bothered to add my father's name to the registry till he was old enough to question his existence. (page 118)

- Choi In Jip, my father/ Paek Un-sŏn, my father's mentor. "Montage is an idea that arises from the collision of independent shots" is from *Film Form* by Sergei Eisenstein, trans. by Jay Leyda (1949, 1977). According to my father, as an act of anti-colonial defiance, Paek manipulated the photo of the Korean marathon winner at the 1936 Berlin Olympics, erasing the Japanese flag on the runner's shirt. The photo appeared on *Dong-A Daily*'s front page. The newspaper was immediately shut down by the Japanese colonial government for several months. After seeing my father's award-winning photo of a Japanese mother and her children in a hurry to flee Seoul when Korea was liberated, Paek recruited my father as a photojournalist for the newspaper. As soon as the Korean War began, Paek asked my father to go with him to a southern province for safety, but my father stayed in Seoul because he couldn't part with his camera, which he had left at the office. Soon after, Paek was recruited to North Korea. My father thinks Paek didn't survive the war. (page 119)

▸ All three photos were taken by my father's colleagues. According to my father, North and South Korean journalists were able to mingle freely at Panmunjom prior to the 1961 military coup led by Park Chung Hee. He pointed out to me which were North Koreans, but I don't remember, and perhaps it is for the best. We are all orphans, after all. From top: February 1958, my father in a wool beanie hat. He is telling a funny story about a joke a UPI bureau chief played on his colleague, that the Korean National Airlines (KNA) was hijacked by North Korea/ October 27, 1958, my father and his North and South Korean colleagues at Panmunjom/ March 3, 1958, my father and his friend Kim Ch'ŏn-gil fooling around at Panmunjom. Both were trying to get to the phone first to call their presses. The quotations in italics, "obtuse/ the third meaning/ the passage from language" and (later) "a signifier without a signified," are from "The Third Meaning" in *Image-Music-Text* by Roland Barthes, trans. by Stephen Heath (1977). (page 120)

▸ The photo at the top shows a painting of Syngman Rhee, the first US-handpicked president of the Republic of Korea—South Korea/ two photos by my father of the April 1960 Student Revolution, which ousted Rhee's anticommunist, corrupt, and authoritarian administration/ a press conference held by American officials, announcing that Rhee had fled the country and martial law had been enforced. My father is in the center with his 16 mm camera. (page 121)

▸ My father doesn't remember which colleague took this photo of him filming this ceremony soon after Park Chung Hee led the coup in May 1961. My father is squatting next to the photographer in a checkered shirt. "A signifier without a signified" is from "The Third Meaning." The man holding the paper on the left is the former US-backed dictator Park Chung Hee. (page 122)

# Acknowledgments

Some of the poems from "Mirror Words" were performed at the Bagley Wright Lecture Series and Wave Books event in September 2016, and some versions of them have appeared in the journals *Cordite Poetry Review* and *Tender*, and in the chapbook *Sky Translation*.

"Ahn Hak-sŏp #1" appeared in *Inherited Trauma* (Annex Series, eohippus labs, 2018).

"Ahn Hak-sŏp #2" and "Ahn Hak-sŏp #3" appeared also in *Sky Translation* (Goodmorning Menagerie, 2019).

"Ahn Hak-sŏp #4" was published as a chapbook (The Green Violin, 2018).

"Ahn Hak-sŏp #5" appeared in *Black Warrior Review*.

"Orphan Kim Gyeong-nam" and "Orphan Jeong Jeong-ja" appeared in *LARB Quarterly Journal*.

"Orphan Heo Jeom-dal," "Orphan Kim Gyeong-nam," "Orphan Yu Gi-myo," and "Orphan Nine" appeared in *Granta*.

"Planetary Translation," "Interpellation of Return," and "(Blue × 300!)" appeared in *Chicago Review*.

Some versions of the paragraphs in "Wings of Return" beginning with "What I remember about my childhood are children . . ." and "In 1980, my father filmed the rising waves . . ." have previously appeared in *Harriet*, the blog for the Poetry Foundation, and in the *Modern Poetry in Translation* issue "The Great Flight."

I am grateful to all the editors of these journals and chapbooks for their support.

I am deeply grateful to Mr. Ahn Hak-sŏp for telling me about his struggles. Even though his friends hoped that I would write an article about Mr. Ahn for prominent newspapers, I believe poetry is more effective as a language of resistance. Poetry can defy erasure. To Ahn Il Soon for kindly introducing me to Mr. Ahn. To Dr. Ahn-Kim Jeong-Ae for her courage and generously sharing her research.

To poet and translator Sasha Dugdale for encouragement and in-depth feedback on "The Orphans." I borrowed "obelus" from one of Sasha's poems about Eric Gill, and Sasha borrowed "oblong" from mine as a way of waving to each other across distance, memory, and language. To Forrest Gander and Valerie Mejer Caso for their enormous hearts and giving me orders to write. To poet friends Sarah Mangold and Melanie Noel in Seattle for always staying close by. To Stephen Hong Sohn for including me in his "team work."

To Joshua Beckman and Heidi Broadhead for believing in me and my work. To Blyss Ervin and Ryo Yamaguchi for their warmth and enthusiasm. To Jeff Clark for his brilliant design. To Charlie Wright without whom Wave Books wouldn't exist. Thank you, Wave Books, for giving me a home, a sanctuary.

To the Lannan Foundation for the 2016 Lannan Literary Fellowship, which enabled me to have time off from work to travel, research, and write. And the Lannan Residency of July 2018 in Marfa, Texas, allowed me to finally weave together everything that I had gathered. Thank you, Martha Jessup and Douglas Humble. And a belated thank you to the Whiting Foundation for having given me the initial incentive to keep persisting as a poet.

To my father for his remarkable sight and memory. To my husband, Jay, for nurturing my wings.